SERENITY

Vol. 1 of the Equilibrium Series

Tammy,

C. D. Clark

Visionary Publishing

Scripture quotations are from the King James Version.

Cover Design by Vesper Media Group L.L.C.

ISBN-13: 978-0999155219

ISBN-10: 0999155210

For my dearest mother.

Dedications

For it is He who receives the highest praise!

First and foremost, I want to thank my family and friends for their continuous support, because you make this possible. This is more than just a book, it's a mission. I want to acknowledge all who inspired me when writing this book. I hope to encourage those who want to write and share their story, may this book motivate you to do so.

The Lord is my shepherd; I shall not want.

2 He maketh me to lie down in green pastures: he leadeth me beside the still waters.

3 He restoreth my soul: he leadeth me in the paths of righteousness for his name's sake.

4 Yea, though I walk through the valley of the shadow of death, I will fear no evil: for thou art

with me; thy rod and thy staff they comfort me.

Psalm 23: 1-4, KJV

Table of Contents

Introduction

We listen to the cries and pleas of the neglected---
shunned by loved ones, casted out by strangers, and left to the
unknown fate of reproach. We lend an ear when others won't.,
together we give voice to them. We rise and begin the battle
from within. We listen to the martyred and to the exploited. We
read the concealed label given that spells troubled and
irrelevant. Together, we give voice to the voiceless – worth to
the worthless – strength to the helpless – love to the loveless –
we take a stand with those identified as troubled, casualties, or
as victims of circumstance. Together we stand, awaken the
numbness from within, and map a framework for all to win.

Discernment

Rise

A distant voice speaks

Stop your worrying, cease your discontentment

Be not fearful of where you are

Greatness is where you will conclude

Rise

Stand upon your feet

He will sweep away from this land,

Desolate destruction caused by man

Havoc will no longer

Inhabit this land

Rise

Remember all His commands

When they ask who has sent you, tell them, *I Am*

When they ask why you have come,

Tell them for the sake of man

For many will pick up their cross

But few will carry it

Rise

The time is nearing

The nearing of His righteous hand

The revealing of the decrees in both books

A great and mighty discernment will come upon this land

Living Waters

I am drifted by your love

I am captivated by your compassion

Take my hand

Trust that I have come as I am

Flawed

Blemished

I am refuged by your faith

I am reserved by your embrace

What an unspoken grasp you have

You have allowed me to be all that I am

Imperfect

Misguided

I am at ease by the sound of your voice

I am at peace knowing you are near

Soul Talk

Tell me your secrets

The ones you want to take to your grave

The secrets that tell

Why fear is in your eyes

The secrets that reveal why

Loneliness is your friend,

Why companionship is your rival

Why love is a stranger and

Why your friends plot revenge

Tell me your secrets

The ones you want to take to your grave

The Prevailing Darkness

Running

Darkness is prevailing

Falling down on my knees

Begging and pleading

But silence steals my ability to speak

In the shadowy darkness

My spirit lurks about

Residing in unspoken places

Running and chasing,

Before it does harm

Where has my sanity gone?

How am I to see when

Darkness is my spirit's keeper

Existence is what is left of me

Running and chasing the remnants of me

Fragments only remain

The Imminent

I ask for mercy

For I am haunted

I am buried by my wrongs

I am overwhelmed

I am in fear

My doings, unforgivable

Not worthy of any mercy

My very being stripped away

Forgotten

Left for the coming judgment

The prevailing darkness

The Redeemer

Shed His blood for me

Died on the cross for me

Sacrificed everything for me

Set me free

Astounding love for me

Immersion in the holy waters,

Washed away my sins

He, who gives strength to the weak

Strength to the broken

Christ, the restorer

For He is first in all my ways

And I stand my ground

He is the Lord Almighty

The Redeemer

Ingenuity

We have to be honest with ourselves

Especially when it hurts the most

Cease looking in the mirror

With thoughts of shame and ridicule

Don't let the words of others,

Words of pain, be yours

Be first to see the divine beauty

In this life of love

This life of sacrifice

This life of transience

Ingenuity

Sacred Endeavors

The life that brings you happiness

The life that brings joyfulness

Sadness

Sorrow

Cannot have its way

No captives for claim

The life that brings gladness

The life that brings peacefulness

Anger

Resentment

Have no crippling effect

No keeping ground for the soul

The life that brings meekness

The life that brings laughter

Shouts of pride

Cries of melancholy

Have no resting place

No voice to corrupt

Breathe

With every breath remember His mercy

The one who bled for you

With every breath dwell on Him

Set your thoughts on the life you've been given to live

Painful memories no longer your captor

With every breath give praise

For there's living breath in you

Breathe...

You're not alone

He is always surrounding you

With every breath, be gracious

For you are loved eternally

Be empowered to unveil it

It has changed your life,

Forever you are changed

In this precious moment, realize,

It is your moment,

It is your time

Breathe

Run Away With Me

To a place we can't be seen

We'll create moments of masterpiece

Lasting an eternity

The rumors,

And the whispers,

Of our secret escapes

Run away with me

Trust that our embrace

Will always be enough

There will be legends told of us

A story told to generations to come

Stories of our inseparableness

Our *lofty* escapes

Run away with me

Let fate determine our outcomes

Perhaps we'll be our own mirage

Let life be the usher of all our fulfillments

Existence

The weight of the world

In the palms of your hands

The weight is a burden

A battle not meant to be won

A game not meant to be played

Diverted by the trials, while

Catastrophe threatens your being

Who had your permission to steal

Your everlasting moments of joy?

Your gleaming laughter

Your hopeful cries

The fire that was in your eyes

The Reflected View

A song so sweet

It is capturing

The melody playing,

It brought me to my knees

Who am I to criticize?

Who am I to ostracize?

Who am I to victimize?

What is this sweetness that

Causes inward reflection

Stripped of all existence of pride

Sent to a place where a mirror is the view

The reflected view

Surrender

To the He who says

You are unholy

The One who says your

Words are vile and unclean

May His mercy fall upon you

To He who says your

Decisions have consequences

The One who will judge all some day

The One who says all have sinned

And fall short of the glory of God

May His grace be upon you

To He who forgives

The One who promised salvation

To He who loves

And His words renew the broken

Desert Storm

The untold story of us

Reflects what has become of us

Our lost and the jilted rewrites

Dances in the cosmic stars

Reflections of *our* night,

Broken by the lies

The red moon

Reflects our bitter heart

Visions in the starry night

The darkness hid our secret escapes,

Our midnights embraced

Where has our unforsaken love vanished?

Haunted by the unknown

And seized by the known

Reaching out knowing rejection follows

Darkness reveals our moments of pain

Desert storm

Unwarranted Persecution

Emerge from captivity

Break the chains of restraint

Rise from the ground

Restore your command

One opportunity

One chance

Even without the chains,

Is your mind your new captor?

Have you decided to remain?

Accustomed to the torment

The treatment of pain

The acceptance of battery

I tug at you

I shout at all remnants of you

Take the given freedom

Leave behind all that remains

Emerge from captivity

Break the chains of restraint

Rise from the ground

Restore your command

Unwarranted persecution

The Revealing Soul

I often wondered if you had cried as much as I had

When your mind was overwhelmed

Your soul was the essence of sorrow, knowing no hope

I often wondered if fear threatened your very existence

When troubles came in the late hours when pillowing your head

When your future was unveiled to never have been in your hands

I often wondered what prevailing thoughts

Were the most constant and unforgettable

When outcomes were uncertain

And the handouts of life were turmoil and pain

What shook your very being,

Raised you out of your slumber,

What brought down the walls of misery and pain?

At what moment had you stepped into the fight?

Any mysteries you still desire to explore,

Any passion left that draws you near?

Secrets to disclose,

Or stories to be told?

Never Far Away

Again and again, I say it now

Let your praise be heard

Let your voice be stretched loud

Again and again, I say it louder

For He is the one you need most

The guidance to break free

From destructive behaviors

Reckless needs

Took you captive

Pulled you closer and closer,

To a destructive reality

Reversible damage

When God took ahold,

His one pull set you free

For you had faith and believed

Faith that God was never far away

Belief in His eternal word

Again and again, I say it now

Let your praise be heard

Let your voice be stretched loud

Again and again, I say it louder

Never far away

Deplorable Implementation

Balanced by fragmented sanity

Mended together in partiality

Gripped by the irrational things

What am I to make of your vain sacrifice?

The exhaust of one's labor is merely forgotten

When yesterdays are all our tomorrows

Life's retaliation has begun its course

Conflicted acts of pain and dolor

Overwhelmed by life's expectancies

A fine line between life and death

Broken paths and unknown journeys

What is to be my response to

Your prideful preparations?

Any splendor left in the

Reversible destruction?

When the now is a broken present

The Act of Revolution

Making a difference does not

Start with an act of the elite

Does not start with telling

Someone else to take lead

It begins with – *us*

Facing who we are, and

Who we have become

We are revealed to be broken inside

Wanting to fix the outside

The wicked neglect of the inside

It's about letting go of pride,

Manipulation,

And the need to control others

The judgmental remarks

Face yourself, before it's too late

And regret is all you see

You are on your knees

Wondering...

If forgiveness is written in

His book of decrees

Have a change of heart,

Rise and make a change

Don't be trapped in selfish ways, and

Cold hearted acts of pain

Be the person He has bestowed you to be

Someone your sons and daughters

Will remember throughout their existence

The act of permutation, transformation

The Employ of Pursuit

What are the depths of my pain?

How far am I willing to go to know?

Is the search endless?

Is the search hopeless?

How am I to address this pain?

An emotion that just won't diminish

All out of tears

All out of cares

All mysteries revealed

All secrets are known

Where am I to hide?

Why am I to hide?

I am visible to the eye

Earthly Decree

What is this that taunts me?

What is this fear?

What is this encumbrance I carry?

No safe haven

Even dreams are invaded

I reach with the expanse of both hands

No one comes to take its grip

For I have dwelled too deep

For the regions I reside, all sanity flees

For I am left to do battles with thyself

Face the remorse I've sowed so deep

Hollowness

The glass is empty

A symbolic representation

Of what I choose not to face

The exasperated calls haunting me

Tormenting me

Whispering, *you're not strong enough*

Too weak to shun

In too deep to walk away

But recognizable even in its indulgence

Giving in to the very thing that destroys

Takes my very being away

Strips me from all sanity

The self – annulled

Hollowness

When Everything Is Not Enough

Exalted by the moment

Captured by His embrace

A revelation revealed to the elect

This is not of my doing,

Not of my choosing

Who am I to take credit

For works I do not own,

Receive gifts never

Meant for me,

Accept praise for ideas

Not my own?

I am owed nothing

Yet, I owe everything

Chain Reaction

The soulful loss of all there is

And all there will ever be

Depravation of the heart

How am I to explain such loss?

When the ultimate reactor is *us*

Here – I stand – in the voids

All there was and all there is left to be

Relied upon the sequence of time

When the hours turn into days

Our present decisions unveiled in the future

Due to the creation of time

Our reaction to such things,

Is it the destined matter of predestination?

Factors my own hand has welded,

And outcomes where fate has its last say

Here – I stand – in a future I don't recognize

A result of a chain reaction

Celestial Fate

Whose mercy have I shunned?

Forgiveness shouldn't be my plagued enemy

Whose adversary have I become?

Dark forces surround me

Whose sins have I embodied?

I'm weighed down by unknown troubles

Whose love have I taken for granted?

I swallow the bitterness I have sowed

Whose dark misfortunes have I inherited?

Innate calamities create barriers

Even seraphs cannot break

Whose conspiracies have I entered?

Unknown schemes emerging

Take a Stand

I don't know if I should take a stand

Will I be the one?

The one who waits,

Maintain my devotion,

My regard

I don't know if I should take a stand

We create moments of glory

Capture memories of beauty

How proverbial, the sound of your voice

Relieved to learn of your benevolent care

I'll be the one,

The one who will take a stand

Reconnect with our love again

The Familiarity of Being

I ceased what I thought would be forever

An abrupt end, followed by regret

A fight my innate fear wouldn't let me join

Afraid of any pain I might endure

A change leading away from my comfort

Misled by the rejection of truth

Discontentment, oh that infernal sin

A revelation of a different ending

The details I never explored

The let of my finite mind, conclude judgment

Scattered emotions ran rampant

The familiarity of being

Enduring Strength

What extent must man suffer?

The labors of pain

The sacrifices forgotten

Hopes whisked away by storms

How deep are the roots of pain?

The drowning of sorrow

The exasperated defeat

The unanswered cries

Forgotten memories

Struggled identities

Left for the unknown

Enduring strength

Light breaks through darkness

The hostile endures, an end has come

The Faith spoken ill and with disregard

Their days are numbered

False tongues have had their last quiver of moments

The beauty of atonement left to the chosen

The uncompromising love

Enduring strength

Trusted Artifice

I lay in my own ambition

What good is success, if it follows destruction

I rest in my own securities

What good is money, if it diagrams a trail of problems

Why tie the knot, when the divorce industry

Sells you propaganda of being alone

I reek of unequivocal laziness

Why mobility, when we're sold convenience

Why pursue a lifetime of wellness,

When they sell temporary life sustaining packages

Dare to Dream

In the wild jungles

You come alive

Your being, your essence

Reveals your hidden desires

You escape to the hidden gallows

Places of the unreturned

The place of the battlefield cries

Not even the boldest of bold

Would dare wander into these regions

In the wild jungles

You come alive

Your being, your essence, returned

Accomplished what

No one dare would

Or even dream they could

Your conquered plights

In the wild jungles

You come alive

Elect Affairs

Wrapped in the arms of love

Rescued in the final moments

By the grip of my hand

I felt the pulse of trust

The heartbeat of empathy

The electrifying touch of autoscopy

Come

Leave all you think you know

Embrace divine conscientiousness

Don't be bound by your measure

The reveals of life are soon to come

Bringing wholeness

Unveiling the sanctity of life

Where reason is defied

And all we knew is left to the forgotten

Elect affairs

Temperament

Sometimes you never appreciate

What you have until it is lost

The hand you want to lend,

Shouldn't be a tight grip

Sacrifice is to be embraced,

Not avoided like plague

Giving is a cost, one should

Not measure its return

Challenge is overcome,

By decisions and actions

The more numb you are to your

Surroundings, pain and suffering,

The more difficult the awakening

Temperament

The Looking Glass

Perspectival shadows down casting a

Traumatic past of unrelenting pain

The disclosed experience of betrayal,

Reveals unforgiveness

The unequivocal fight of self-denial

The mirroring view of agony,

Reflection of our imperfections

The battle cry of iniquities

The struggles of identities

The smiles that hide our sufferings

Traumatized by your surroundings

The walk among thunderstorms of vanity

The Looking Glass

Little Girl, Little Girl

Little girl, little girl

Don't be sad

Don't let your heart be troubled

Little girl, little girl

Come out to play

Don't be afraid of everything

All will be ok

Little girl, little girl

Fear not what you've yet to understand

I know life can be mysterious,

Hold steadfast to its moments of glory

Little girl, little girl

You're in the best years of your life

All responsibilities left to those beyond your age

Little girl, little girl

A Stir of Echoes

You are in a dark room

Surrounded by unknown voices

You hear whispers and echoes

Fear is gripping you

Echoes in the wind

Telling secrets of your insanity

Did you really think you would

Get away with what you did?

You fear God is whispering

Speaking of eternal things,

The fall of man and his state of being

You turn to the scriptures

And the first word you see,

Is the word *repent*

The Songs of Angels

I hear the voices of angels sing

I feel my heavy, troubled soul find peace

My weakened and frail body

Once again can stand firm on two feet

The battles I have lost,

I no longer pay the price

The mental prisons I inhabit,

No longer my mind's keeper

I hear the voices of angels sing

My eternal being has risen again

The framework of my heart connected

Again to the one true King

My soul set free

My rhythm matches a heavenly beat

Fear isn't the formula of my approach

My need of forgiveness is all I bring

I hear the voices of angels sing

The free gift of grace sets my internal framework free